Healing A-Z

The Words
That Can Heal
Body, Mind
and Spirit

Jimmy Mack

Healing Body, Mind and Spirit, People,
Places, Things, Pets and Situations

Healing A-Z
The Words That Can Heal Body, Mind and Spirit

ISBN: 978-1-5408-1172-1
(Also available for Kindle)

Book design & page layout: Lighthouse24
Cover image: Carlos Amarillo / Shutterstock

Sidney Kilgore Esq (sidneywkilgorepa@gmail.com)
Trademark/Patents Advice

Sandy Bidinger (Sandy.bidinger@gmail.com)
Promotions, Marketing & Sales
www.smbeconnected.com

Hunter McKeown (huntermzk@yahoo.com)
Audio/Visual/App Edits

Jack Furlong (JohndFurlong@gmail.com)
Web Design & Support
http://www.johndfurlong.com

Notice of Informed Consent

I certify that I will consult my health care practitioner regarding any intuitive, spiritual, holistic or alternative treatment I may receive. I fully understand that Intuitive Medical Readings or any kind of energy based counseling or service received through this book is in NO way a substitute for my medical consultations or treatments from my medical doctor (s) or any licensed health care professional(s).

Disclaimer

All the information in this book is published in good faith and for general information purpose only. We do not make any warranties about the completeness, reliability and accuracy of this information. Any action you take upon the information you find in this book, is strictly at your own risk. we will not be liable for any losses and/or damages perceived as arising from the use of this book.

From this book you can visit other websites by following hyperlinks to such external sites. While we strive to provide only quality links to useful and ethical websites, we have no control over the content and nature of these sites. These links to other websites do not imply a recommendation for all the content found on these sites. Site owners and content may change without notice and may occur before we can remove a link which may have gone 'bad'.

Please be also aware that when you leave our website, other sites may have different privacy policies and terms which are beyond our control. Please be sure to check the Privacy Policies of these sites as well as their "Terms of Service" before engaging in any business or downloading or uploading any information.

This entire book and its concepts revolve around prayer.
Super Charged turbo charged prayers!

Special thanks to:
Jacie Lara Gamez RN
Certified Veterinarian Technician
for inspiring me and pushing me
to complete this project

Contents

Introduction

IN THIS BOOK, you will find topics of disease, illness, and disorders of the body, mind and spirit. It is written as if each one were pertaining to you so that you can work on you. Obviously, you can use this book to work on others and it is intended as a guide for you with topical suggestions. You will want to make certain you are clear, yes, unclear, no and running forward prior to doing any work in this book. The same holds true of someone who you may be praying over or on. They do not need to be present. You can work on them or with them remotely, at any time of the day or night, 24/7 the same as you do by saying prayers. Please know, that these are suggestions. As you read this now, it is my sincere wish and hope that you will be divinely guided and shown the ideal words and concepts that will allow you to get to the bottom of and vastly improve any health challenge.

Always keep everything as simple as possible. Yes or No. Positive or Negative. Strong or Weak. Heavy or light. Whenever you doubt or are uncertain, go with simple. Your words and concepts will be different than mine. Words and concepts of others will be different from ours. You will want to be accepting and understanding of this. Utilizing custom words and phrases will generate greater responses, and better magical outcomes. As always, you will want to be hydrated and use a pendulum or standing applied kinesiology. Feelings of heavy or light, or using your fingers. Any acceptable way for you to differentiate between positive, negative, yes or no. Once you are there, you will need to use **www.myliquidfish.com** Change Made Simple®, so that you can spiritually change the position to your ideal outcome. Things can be negative or positive. Bad things can show as strong positives, as can something that is negative and weak can also be a strong yes. The same meaning can be found where something that is good can be lacking.

Please know that all these words, diseases, illnesses and disorders are to act as only a direction for you to consider. You will want to cross reference and test a lot of different angles to any one of these words that are in here A through Z.

For instance, as an example:

- **Annoyances** (can be spouse, parents, children, in-laws, coworkers, bosses etc.).
- **Disappointments** (Desires, Needs and Wants that never materialized),
- **Doubts** (About what you have done in the past or will do in the future).
- **Frustrations** (Over any and everything).
- **Grievances** (Abuse, betrayal, blame, and having been treated unfairly or wrongfully).
- **Hurts** (Criticized, loss, lack of appreciation, love and support).
- **Indecisiveness** (Inability to handle undesirable situations).
- **Regrets** (regarding decisions made, actions taken, or choices selected).
- **Rejections** (personally or work related).
- **Stresses** (Health, financial or relationship).
- **Worries** (Past, present or future security).

Additional words:

- **Ancestral**
- **Culture**
- **DNA**
- **Environmental**
- **External**
- **Family**
- **Fitness**
- **Health**
- **Integration inside**
- **Integration outside**
- **Karma**
- **Negative**
- **Positive**
- **Perceptions**
- **Prosperity**
- **Religion**
- **Strength**
- **Weakness**

You will literally need to test these words, or cross match them with your disease, illness or disorder. See how they test. If you are hung up on arthritis related to your DNA or ancestral or family pattern you will fish it out. Any one of the above or for mentioned words could be a game changer in your disease, illness, disorder or challenge. It will not matter to me what your healthcare provider may have written in your chart, such as "patient has arthritis" because after using MyLiquidFish® and this book you may miraculously wind up with no symptoms, proving then it was all worth it.

You should also want to cross reference any prescription medications or herbs you may be taking to see if they test strong or weak. Ideally you will want to be able to take them with zero side effects and I believe that is possible. So, if you hold a medication for your arthritis for example, and it pulls you backwards for weakness, fish out from the bottom left whatever that is until your medication test positive for you. I believe it is possible to combine western medicine with spiritual prayer and healing processes for the best of both worlds.

The word negative pathogens include bacteria, virus, mold, fungus, mildew, yeast, candida, and parasites. One or more of these or a mixture of these could be the culprit preventing health and healing.

Research Jim Humble at **www.jimhumble.org** *as a suggestion.*

As always, this should not be used in replacement for professional medical treatment. Please seek help immediately if you are experiencing a life-threatening problem.

Abdominal Cramps – Due to fear of letting go. Safety and comfort allow me to trust and let go.

Abscess – Due to regrets, over-thinking, resentments keeping us stuck. Releasing the past allows me to have peace, and to let go of past hurts.

Accidents – Due to feeling violent, challenging authority, and stuffing instead of speaking up. It is safe and comfortable for me to speak up without fear of reprisal allowing me to be at peace.

Aches – Due to stuck energy, and longing for better. It is safe and comfortable to love and be loved.

Acne/Blackheads/Pimples – Due to the inability to accept myself and others. I feel grounded and accepting of myself and others while at peace, here and now.

Addictions – Due to evading of self, and unrealistic expectations, uncertainty about self–awareness. It is safe and comfortable to enjoy myself and I am accepting of myself. I am enough.

Addison's Disease – Due to anger, and nutritional lack, emotional deprivation. With love, my body, mind, spirit and emotions are in harmony with each other. My soul is satisfied.

Adenoids – Due to feelings of being unloved, family friction and discord. Inability to know one's place in the family. I am loved. Welcomed. Accepted.

Adrenal Problems – Due to anxiety about feeling defeated. Apathy about self-care. It is safe and comfortable to love and care for myself and to allow others to care for me as well.

Aging Problems – Due to inability to live in the present, rejection of self and others. Inability to be fully present. My being and my life are ageless. I will continue my journey with love in my heart, regardless of past present and future.

Aids – Due to feeling guilty about sex. Shame and down on self. Incapable of being more. I now feel capable of loving and appreciating my life. I feel as one with the Universe.

Alcoholism – Due to feeling dejected, hopeless and sad. What is the use? I am accepting of myself, here in the now. I am deserving of receiving love. I am worthy and whole.

Allergies – Due to denial of the self's own power. Allergic to self. Allergic to everything. I am at a neutral place with neither hard charges for or against anything.

Alzheimer's Disease – Due to an inability to accept the world and the current or present situation. Feelings of anger and helplessness, daily. By releasing the past I forgive, and forget, and move into joy and align my brain at 100% efficiency.

Amenorrhea – Due to disliking one's self and the female gender. I am accepting of my gender, and all body functions flow with grace and ease.

Amnesia – Due to inability to take a stand. Escapism that feeds on fear. It is safe and comfortable to realize I can access universal information at any time. Safely and effectively.

Amyotrophic Lateral Sclerosis (Lou Gehrig's Disease) – Due to denial. Feelings of failure. Unable to accept self-worth. It is safe for me to succeed. I am worthy of success. I am in love with life. I have released this disease.

Anaphylaxis (Allergic Reactions, Severe) –

Anemia – Due to insufficient happiness, and bad attitude. Starting and stopping abruptly. Inability to be smooth. I am full of joy and have the ability and capacity to maintain it.

Angioedema – see *Facial Swelling*.

Ankles – (Check and clear weak foundations) Due to instability and inability to be grounded and to stop on a dime. Lack of direction. I feel grounded. I know intuitively when to change direction. I am feeling supported.

Anorexia – Due to rejection love for self and others, and the inability to accept nurturing, or anything that is good. Pushing away. I accept myself for who I am. I allow nurturing and nourishment for my body, mind and spirit. I am nourished, whole and complete.

Anus/Anal Disorders – (Check and clear abscess, bleeding, fistula, itching, pain) Due to inability to release, let go, and discharge waste. Feeling stuck and ungrounded or like a kite in the wind, indecision. Inability to accept nutrition and nurturing. Feeling dumped on. I release that which is no longer of service to me. It is safe to let go. My body allows releasing from the haunting of the past. I am releasing all with love as I come into being fully present, here and now.

Anxiety – Due to the inability to trust in the flow of life. I acknowledge that spirit loves me. I allow comfort, safety and joy to envelope me now.

Apathy – Due to fear of the inability to feel and be fully present and productive. I experience life with grace and ease. I open myself up to the wonders of life and living. I engage in forward motion.

Appendicitis – Due to blockage and fear. Lack of nourishing blood flow. I allow life to flow threw me joyously as I smoothly meditate in the present moment.

Appetite Loss or Excess – Due to raging fear and the inability to trust, emotional instability and obsessing over upsets. Normality and safety comfort and envelope me now. The theme of smooth rules the day bringing safety, peace and joy.

Arms – Due to weakness preventing the ability to hold capacity for life. It is safe and comfortable to lovingly hold all aspects of life with ease.

Arterial Disorders – Due to blocking of the ability of flowing joy in one's life. Spirit fills my heart with joy and love flows through my arteries and veins.

Arteriosclerosis – Due to being stuck, and the inability to see positively. Having a narrowed focus and inability to resolve or accept another's point of view. Inability to meet in the middle. I allow choice and acceptance of love and others points of view.

Arthritis – (Check and clear weak joints and inflammation) Due to an inability to resolve, and blaming others outside of one's self. Excessive criticism and judgement. I approve of myself. I love and accept love. I realize and believe in choices and accept others points of view without judgement or criticism.

Asphyxiating Attacks/Airway – Due to being stuck. Inability to trust the flow of life. For children, it is the inability to be heard. I feel safe in my part of the world and in the flow of life.

Asthma – Due to stuffy feelings and suppressed tears of sorrow or sadness. Inability to breath in and enjoy life. I feel cherished, safe, loved as I breath in the breath of life. I am nourished.

Athlete's Foot – Due to frustrations with life. Inability to be dry. Dampness. Fungus. It is easy to be warm and dry. I feel loved and loving and move with grace and ease.

Autoimmune Disorders – (Check and clear bacteria, candida, parasites and allergies to one's self) Due to self-sabotage and attacking of one's self. Shirking one's responsibilities to life, ducking out. I am fully aligned and integrated in this life. This body, mind, and spirit are all on track. *Research anti-inflammatories such as turmeric.*

Back – Due to lack of feelings of support in life. I believe, think, know and feel the universe will always support me.

Back Problems – Due to fear of instability, lack of financial support, and fear of emotional support. As I say this now, I allow the universe to come threw me, creating support in knowing that I am supported in every aspect of my life.

Bad Breath – Due to feelings of resentment and revenge overflowing into the here and now. I will now choose the voice of love and kindness. I release all anger, resentment, and karmic debt up into the universe.

Balance Problems – Due to inability to focus thoughts and though processes, as well as the ability to use common sense. I feel centered and coming from a place of neutrality I am in allowance of safety and balance to flow through me now. I am grounded.

Baldness – Due to lack of trust in the universal process of life, and loss of control over oneself. I choose acceptance of myself and in the process of life. I love and accept myself and the universal plan. It is safe and comfortable for me to flourish.

Bed-Wetting – Due to parental fears and feelings of making the wrong choices. Each child is accepted individually by the universe. Each child is loved and cherished by each parent.

Belching/Excessive Burping – Due to a lack digestive enzymes and racing through life. I am developing the ideal pace in my life. There is more than enough time for everything I need to do.

Bell's Palsy – (Check traumatic events, past karma and stuffing feelings.) Due to inability to express one's self for fear of being wrong. I forgive myself and others. It is safe and comfortable for me to speak up.

Bites – Animal or Bug-Due to anger and fear towards animals, and fear coming from the animal. Bothersome, tiny things, and excessive amounts of annoyance. I release myself from irradiate behaviors and reverse polarity. I now run direct and I am safe.

Bladder Disorders – (Check and clear if you are pissed off) Due to an inability to store or let go, and not knowing the difference. It is safe and comfortable to release what no longer serves me and to take in the renewed sense of wellbeing.

Bleeding Disorders – (Check blood is weak or blood is strong) Due to an inability to have communications with grace and ease between all organs, glands and systems. I joyfully express life and living, communications are filled with grace and ease here and now.

Bleeding of the Gums – (Check strength of gums) Due to stuffing and fear, with an inability to express. My teeth, gums, and jaw are all in symphony with one another.

Blisters – Due to rubbing people the wrong way. Going too fast and doing too much. I am in the flow of life and I know there will be more than enough time to complete everything.

Blood Disorders – Due to stagnant energy, stuck ideas, lack of joyfulness. The circulation of rich, colorful and enriching ideas flow threw me now.

Blood Pressure – Due to problems with emotional hurts, family dilemmas, being out of the flow of life. The past is now released, harmony flows in, around and threw my veins and arteries. Balance is the theme of the day.

Boils – Due to the inability to express anger and a need to release impurities. Ease, joy and glory flow in around me now. I am clean.

Bone Disorders/Fractures – Due to the inability to get along within the organized system. An inability to comply with direction.

Bone Marrow – (Check strengthening bone marrow cells) Due to lack of support and nourishment in one's life. Springing forward the inspiration of life's renewal. Life nourishes me.

Bowel Disorders – Due to a holding onto waste in life and a fear of letting go. I now release what serves me no longer.

Brain Disorders – Due to a malfunction in the computer with scattered data that could be released by downloading the 2.0 software version of the brain. With grace and ease, I download the 2.0 version into the computer of my mind, reprogramming it now. *Research Bulletproof coffee, and Gaba and lithium orotate supplements. Fish oils as well.*

Breast Disorders (Lumps, Cysts, Mastitis) – Due to putting everyone else before me. Lack of nourishing one's self. Love and joy nourishes us all now. I am just as important as everyone else. I matter. I count.

Breast Cancer – Check virus, bacteria, mold, yeast, parasites. Due to one or more of these combinations. Life nourishes me, and my breasts are 100% healthy and strong.

Breathing Disorders – Due to the inability to take life in to the fullest and feeling undeserving of existence. I take in life fully now. I count and matter, there is a reason for my existence.

Bright's Disease (Nephritis, Kidneys) – Due to inability to feel worthy, deserving or open to receiving. I am enough, my life matters, and all my organs glands and systems are in coherence with one another and function at 100%.

Bronchitis – Due to inflammation of the self and family or family member. Feeling exacerbated. Joy and communications flow in and around my family. Breathing becomes unobstructed and easy for me.

Bruises – Due to self-sabotage, lack of control in life, and a lack of magnesium. My electrolytes are in balance and I flow easily and effortlessly.

Bulimia – Due to an extreme self-loathing and stuffing of one's feelings. Lack of nurturing. Life loves, nourishes and supports me. It is safe and comfortable to be myself.

Burns, Accidental – Due to erratic behavior, being accident prone, and the inability to be at the right temperature. My energy now runs direct; all my temperatures are at the ideal levels that are safe and comfortable for me.

Bursitis (Bursa Inflammation, Gout) – Due to repressed emotions, inability to act out and an inability to defend one's self or holding on to anger. I lovingly release stagnant energy now and bring calm healing onto me now. (Check that bursitis equals weak, and check current supplements that quell inflammation)

Callouses – Due to repetitive motion and fears becoming solidified. Hardened outlooks and ideas. My way or the highway. I am open and receptive to fresh new ideas. I realize there is more than one way.

Cancer – (Check bacteria, mold, mildew, yeast, bacteria and parasites) Due to deep hatreds and resentments, anguish, and overly worrying. I experience life renewed now. There is hope as my cancer tests weak or no and 100% health test positive. I say yes to life.

Candida/Yeast – Due to being scattered, tattered and torn. Disruptions and erratic diet. I give myself permission to heal and to be whole. Candida releases from me now.

Canker Sores – Due to blaming others and an inability to speak up, and smoldering hurts unspoken. In my world, it is now safe and comfortable to speak up and I am heard. 100% health flows threw me now.

Car Sickness – Due to fear of entrapment and feelings of being held down and captive. It is safe and comfortable to allow myself to move through space and time healthy and whole.

Carpel-Tunnel Syndrome – Due to life passing by and feelings of being overworked. Repetitive motions. Check tendons for weakness. Ease, joy and freedom of movement flow through my veins and arteries, tendons and joints as I read this now.

Cataracts – (Check eyes, optical nerves, and brain for weakness) Due to an inability to see clearly and darkness overshadowing the light of my vision. Healing light and frequencies come upon me now. My eyes, optical nerves, and brain function at 100%.

Cellulite – Due to punishing one's self and holding anger about it. I forgive, circulation flows in, around and through me now.

Cerebral Palsy – (Change to weak, or no twice a day) Due to an inability for family to interact with grace and ease. Actions, feelings and influence allow the children and the family to communicate with love, grace and ease. Harmony rules the day.

Childhood Diseases – (Check and clear past lives) Due to left over from past lives, family, DNA, heredity and ancestral disputes. We release these past problems of disease, illness and disorders that are flowing over. WE have learned all the lessons we needed to learn from them and we are released of service to them. A healthy body comes upon us now.

Chills – Due to an inability to regulate temperature and being in the ideal place and time. I feel protected and my temperature is regulated. Everything is well, here and now.

Cholesterol Abnormities – Due to the clogging of open channels and lack of communication in the body. All my body's chemistry is within balance now. All organs and systems process with grace and ease.

Cholelithiasis – see *Gallstones*.

Charlie Horse – see *Cramps*. (Clear this word.) *Research deficiencies in potassium and high magnesium.*

Chronic Diseases – Due to being stuck in the past and an inability to change the future or to be fully present here and now. It is safe and comfortable for me to grow and change. I release the past and I am grounded in the present. I am excited about my future.

Circulatory Disorders – (Check and fish out weak circulation) Due to the inability to go with the ebb and flow of life. The love of life circulates, in, around, and through me now at the right amount of pressure and ease.

Cold Sores – (Check and clear viruses) Due to the inability to speak up and anger boiling within. I hear peaceful words when I express peace in return.

Colds – (Check viral or bacterial) Due to being overwhelmed and needing to shut down. Can often be an excuse to stay out of participating in work or play. I have learned all the lessons I needed to from this cold and release myself from the service to it. I reengage in life and living now.

Colic – Due to overstimulation with surrounding that are annoying at every turn. I am praying as I say and or read this now that colic is released into the void of all that is. In its place, health and wellness flow.

Colon – (Check "my colon is weak", fish until it is strong) Due to the past still haunting me and being hard to let go of. It is safe and comfortable to release the past and to let go here, now.

Colitis – (Check and clear/fish out colitis being strong) Due to being jittery, insecure and imbalanced. All my body's systems are healthy and whole, operating efficiently and in the proper order.

Coma – (Fish from strong to weak) Due to unsuccessful attempt to escape, and being caught in the in-between. It is safe and comfortable to be fully present in this body. All my senses are high functioning here and now.

Concussion – (Fish out to weak or no) Due to being stuck and an inability to engage "offline". I snap back into free communication between body, mind and spirit. I function effortlessly with every breath.

Congestion – (Check viral, bacterial and dampness) Due to weather and overexposure. It is safe and comfortable to release congestion now from this system. I breath in health and well-being as I hear or read this now.

Congenital Disease – (Fish out any positive or yes) Due to a stagnated inability to grow and move forward. I grow and process at a normal rate. Expansive health flows in around and through me now.

Conjunctivitis – (Fish out bacteria) Due to frustration with what is being seen. *Research natural eye drops, I see clearly with grace and ease, and all is well.*

COPD – Due to bronchial weakness, check heart weakness, fish out viral, bacteria, mold, fungus, mildew, yeast, parasites and any negative pathogen. Fish out any negative side effects of medications. I align myself with all medications, herbs and supplements, taking in only their positives. I release any side effects or negative outcomes. I breath in the breath of life and every organ gland and system functions with grace and ease.

Constipation – (Fish to weak) Due to living in the past, being unforgiving and the inability to let go. As I release that which no longer serves me I am nourished by all that which is new. The natural rhythm remains.

Coronary Thrombosis – (Fish out until weak) Due to feelings of inadequacy and being left out, left behind or isolated. I feel supported by the universe and my blood, veins and arteries function at the highest level of smooth.

Coughs – (Fish to no) Due to the feeling of needing to be noticed even if it is by means of disruption. Only the highest and best notices me whether I speak or whether I am in silence. I need not cause a fuss.

Cramps – Due to underlying tension and stress, as well as an inability to let go. Peace comes upon me now. I release and let go and let God. I am hydrated and water flows through me.

Crohn's Disease (Ileitis) – (Check inflammation, and allergies to life, one's self and nutrition) Due to bowels feeling inflamed and being unable to absorb the nutrients of life. It is safe and comfortable to nourish one's self and absorb the best life offers.

Croup (Bronchitis) – Due to a barking cough, child, holding in air. Check bacteria and make sure it is weak. It is safe and comfortable to be calm and let go.

Crying – (Check feelings and upsets for sadness, happiness, crying will pass) Due to sadness or fear. A block in the flow of joy in life. Need for a cleansing. My emotions are stable; I love and approve of myself and others.

Cushing's Disease – Due to overrunning feelings of being overpowered and crushed. I will choose thoughts that improve my mood and outlook about life. I release crushing feelings and emotions. Inspiration for music and art rule the day.

Cuts – (Don't run with knives) Due to hazardous behavior. Erratic and falling outside of the rules. Healing comes upon me now. My own natural processes of my body, including clotting come to my defense.

Cysts – Due to false growths and hurts that are not even ours. Holding on to that which no longer serves us. I release and let go of that which serves me no longer. Everything is well. My past is healed and resolved.

Cystic Fibrosis – (Check bacterial, candida, parasites and negative pathogens, shift DNA to weakness for it) Due to feelings of sorry for one's self. Overwhelmed by life's lessons. Stuck in the inability to move.

Cystitis – (Check bladder, fish out virus, mold, fungus, mildew, parasites and negative pathogens) Due to holding on to inflammation and all that which is no longer of service to us. I release all negativity and I allow pure, clean water to release all the negative pathogens out of this body now.

Deafness/Hearing Impairment – Due to shutting down, stubbornness and the need to be or feel isolated. It is safe and comfortable to hear the positive, heavenly music of this Earth plan and all others.

Dementia – (Check brain for weakness, explore the use of fish oils and supplements including gingko) Due to checking out. An inability to deal with situations as they are presenting themselves as now. My brain functions fully and at 100% and test strong in relation to the rest of my body, spirit and the world.

Depression – see *Psychiatric Illness* (Check and clear brain imbalance and fish out any) Due to unbearable hopelessness. Listlessness. Forlorn. By listening to great music, enjoying arts and exercise, and getting out into the world, I am revived. *Research St. Johns Wart, passion flower, and magnolia or relora bark.*

Diabetes Type 1 – (Check and clear autoimmune and fish out any negativity. Strengthen weak pancreas) Due to allergies to insulin, blood sugar, and weak pancreas. Holding on to. I enjoy the sweetness of life in the correct amounts without being overwhelmed. I live a life that is balanced.

Diabetes Type 2 – Due to anger towards oneself. Inability to process sugar. Allergies to sugar, insulin and one's own blood. Allergic to one's own life. Every day in every way my life improves. The chemistry of my body is in balance. All my organs gland and systems function at 100% efficiency.

Diarrhea – (Check bacteria, parasites and candida) Due to a runoff of ideas. The inability to solidify and process with grace and ease. I am at peace, and process and assimilate with grace and ease.

Delirium – (Check virus and UTI and cystitis) Due to confused and off kilter ideas. Being off my path. My brain functions at 100% and is in harmony with my central nervous system, organs, glands and systems. My kidneys function at 100%.

Dizziness – (Check ADD and ADHD fish to no and clear) Due to scattered, tattered and torn inability to concentrate. I feel grounded, joyful, centered and it is safe and comfortable to be at peace.

Dry Eye – (Check eyes, optic nerve and brain) Due to an inability to see with love or forgive. Unable to clear hurts from the past. I see clearly, with two eyes of love and understanding.

Dysentery – Due to hopelessness, worry and paranoia about people being out to get you. I am steadfast resolute in my life's mission. I am part of a greater whole.

Dysmenorrhea – (Check and clear blood) Due to an underlying gender unhappiness. Sadness. Womanly fears and inability to process life. All my bodily processes function at the highest levels with grace and ease and in harmony with one another.

Earache – (Check and strengthen each ear component. Check brain) Due to parental arguments, past or present, causing turmoil and the want to shut down. I listen with goodness; the earth sings to me. *Research Similasan ear drops.*

Ears Disorders – Due to the want to shut down and shut out words that offend me. Things I don't want to hear or do. I listen with love and invite change.

Eczema – (Check liver and strengthen) Due to antagonisms, irritated at life's basic obstacles. Love and joy envelope me. I feel soothed.

Edema – (Check left sided heart valves and strengthen all) Due to an inability to release that which serves us no longer. It is safe and comfortable for me to release in peace and understanding.

Emphysema – (Check alveoli in and around lungs, strengthen) Due to feeling unworthy. Sorrow. It is safe and comfortable to breathe clearly and freely and to give and receive love with equal measure.

Endometriosis – Due to frustrations and allergies to one's own body and reproductive systems. Allergic to hormones. I am joyous in my female skin. It is safe and comfortable to be me. I am part of the Goddess of the divine.

Enuresis – see *Bedwetting.*

Epilepsy – (Check and clear seizures, fish daily to no, strengthen brain connectivity and processing) Due to life rejection. Everything being struggle, and a deep fear of violence. Life unfolds before me with joy and love.

Epstein-Barr Virus (Mono) – (Check and clear viruses and fish to no) Due to being fatigued, drained and lethargic with life. Washed out. Joy and ease come upon my life now. Energy fills me and functioning is easy.

Eye Disorders – (Check eye functions, optic nerves, muscles, ligaments, and pressures) Due to what you see being displeasing. I see clearly with grace and ease. My eyes function in harmony with my optic nerves and brain.

> **Astigmatism**-Due to misshapen and an out of balance life. Every aspect of my eyes is balanced and in focus. I am free and clear.

> **Cataracts** – Due to natural clouding over to protect my eyes by wearing a coat over them to shield me. I see clearly, and it is safe and comfortable for me to see.

> **Glaucoma** – Due to overwhelming pressure from everyone and everything. All my fluids, pulses, and pressures are at the ideal number. I see with grace and ease as I read or hear this now.

> *Research mineral deficiencies, eye supplements, research indium. Lutein, Bilberry.*

Facial Swelling (Angioedema) – (Check medications, allergic reactions, insects, and past life's. Clear these) Due to inflammation, fluids out of balance and allergies to life. Everything is in balance and in harmony with my body systems.

Fainting – (Check blood pressures, circulation through the heart and brain) Due to the inability to cope with life's pressures. I access unlimited power and this sustains me by keeping me in balance.

Fat/Overweight/Obesity – Due to anger about being denied, self-loathing, stuffing. Feeling powerless and in search of the need for protection and finding only food as comfort. Strengthen the ability to exercise, and eat right correctly for my body. My digestive enzymes and fat emulsifiers are in harmony. I release that which serves me no longer. I find comfort on my own terms. *Research Sunflower lecithin and Safflower Oil supplementation.*

Fatigue – Due to lack of love for what one does in life, and a lack of passion and excitement. Loss of zest in life. Enthusiasm comes upon me now as I reengage in life I regain energy.

Feet Disorders – (Clear weaknesses in joints) Due to lack of structure, inability to move forward in life. Inability to be grounded, and feeling unsafe and unbalanced. With each step, I take, structure and comfort reach up to me. My path is assured. Everything is well. *Research orthotics.*

Female Problems – Due to rejection of self and others. Rejection of gender and sadness over gender assignment. I feel nurtured by the goddess of life and embrace my gender and love being a woman.

Fever – {Check virus and bacteria, and the inability to regulate temperature) Due to seething resentment boiling underneath the surface. Love heals all, and my temperature is regulated even and consistent. *Research tepid bath or shower, acupuncture, and thumb prick solution.*

Fever Blisters – (Check viral and bacterial, strengthen liver and blood) Due to negativity boiling on the surface, deep seeded resentment and long standing negative beliefs. I release heat and resentment with love and longstanding festering is quelled with peace.

Fibroid Tumors – (Check and strengthen hormonal weaknesses, strengthen the flow of life) Due to hurts that won't heal and a bruised ego in relationships. It is safe and comfortable to create life regardless of age.

Fingers, Pain, Inflammation –

Thumb: Worry

Index: Fear

Middle: Sexuality

Ring: Grief

Little: Pretending and control

I release and let go of all pain, inflammation, drama and chaos fall at the waste side I am capable, happy and whole.

Fistula – Due to a fear of letting go. Blocking of final resolutions. It is safe and comfortable for me to engage in the process of life from beginning to end without fear of pain.

Flatulence – (Check digestive enzymes) Due to gulping and swallowing without fully chewing. I process food, nutrients, and fluids with grace and ease and zero side effects.

Flu – see *Influenza*.

Food Poisoning – (Check bacteria, fish out allergic reactions) Due to an inability to defend one's self. Allergic reactions. My body comes online safely, energetically, and in harmony. Brain heart and all systems are restored.

Foot – see *Feet Disorders*.

Fractures – Due to snapping, incomplete and an inability to bond systems. All aspects of my body come together to form a greater whole.

Frigidity – (Check past lives for sexual punishment, karmic slave or master) Due to denial of pleasure, seeing sex as bad. Guilt in pleasing one's self. I release, let go, and it is safe and comfortable to experience love, passion, joy and ecstasy.

Fungal Infections – (Check and clear fungus until it is weak and no) Due to stagnation and being stuck in the past with an inability to let go. Joyously, I experience life. I am complete and have well-being.

Furuncle – see *Boils*.

G

Gallstones (Cholelithiasis) – (Check liver and gallbladder functions, fish out and strengthen systems.) Due to resentment and frustration and commendation. Negative thoughts and stuffing them. An inability to express, and a need to harbor resentment. I process nutrition with grace and ease. I release frustration and resentment. I host only joy and love. *Research Coca-Cola gallbladder cleanse or supplemental cleanses. Research digestive enzymes and ox-bile.*

Gangrene – (Check allergies to one's self, and attacking of one's self.) Due to dark thoughts keeping us stuck, fear of conversations about death. All aspects of this body are filled with grace and ease and 100% healthy, full and whole now. (If this tests weak, fish it to strong.)

Gas Pains – (Check digestive enzymes and chew food more, gulping air and eating too fast are obvious causes) Due to the holding onto of thought and under digested ideologies. It is safe and comfortable to slow down and digest life with grace and ease.

Gastritis – (Check digestive enzymes and water intake) Due to nervous tension, fear, restlessness and uncertainty. I digest life with grace and ease. All my organs, glands and systems are in harmony.

Genital Problems – (Check thriving and virility) Due to masculine and feminine reproduction, creation of life weaknesses. It is safe and comfortable to be strong, aware and moving forward with purpose. Sturdiness of the constitution. Strong fertility comes upon me now.

Glands – Due to way stations, exchanges and activity of sending and receiving. All my organs, glands and systems function at 100% efficiency here and now.

Glandular Fever – see *Mononucleosis.*

Glandular Problems – Due to ideas processing too slowly and a feeling of lethargy and feeling held down by stockiness. Too grounded and sloth like. It is safe and comfortable to be in the present while moving into the future without worrying about the past with grace and ease.

Globus Hystericus – see *Lump in Throat.*

Goiter – (Check all glands and strengthen thyroid, check bacteria, candida and parasites) Due to victimhood. Feeling slighted and attacked by others and self. I stand on my own power, disease, illness and disorder free. It is safe and comfortable to be healthy here and now.

Gonorrhea – (Check bacteria and virus) Due to shame and accusing one's self of being bad as well as allowing others to accuse me of being a bad person too. It is safe and comfortable to love myself and this body. Sex is natural and fun and carefree. Fish to yes if this is no.

Gout – (Check impurities, and joint inflammation) Due to feeling impatient, angry, dominating others in conversations. It is safe and comfortable to communicate with grace and ease with others as well as myself and to be in harmony with everyone.

Grey Hair – (Check mineral deficiencies) Due to internalization of stress, and internal and external pressures. Life is being renewed and refreshed. I am ageless, timeless, and capable of accomplishing anything. *Research Indium.*

Growth Problems/Challenges – Due to being stuck in the past and an inability to move forward. It is safe and comfortable to move forward with grace and ease and to flourish in the present while envisioning a brighter future.

Gum Problems/Bleeding – (Check bacteria and allergies to one's own blood and gums) Due to indecisiveness and the inability to move forward. Inability to hold on. It is safe and comfortable to hang on to what I have now while moving progressively forward. I am deserving.

Fish various colors of mouthwash and use what tests best for you, up to five times a day along with flossing.

Guillain-Barr Syndrome – (Check and clear viral infections) Due to the shutting down of nerves in the body because of complacency and giving up. Every day and every way, my body heals and becomes healthier. I am free of disease illness and disorder.

Halitosis – see *Bad Breath*

Hands Problems/Challenges – (Check joints, and fish out any blocks) Due to stiffness of thought and inability to hold on or let go. Ease, joy and comfort sooth my touch as I read or hear this now.

Hay Fever – Due to allergies of one's self and the change of season. Being out of the flow of life and out of sync with life. I am in the flow of life. Comfort and safety allow me to breath easily and effortlessly.

Headaches – (Check hydration, overthinking, blood flow and pressure) Due to fear of coitizing one's self and hearing it from others. Stockiness. Grace and ease flows in, around and threw me. My brain, heart and central nervous system, organs and glands function together as one. Balance comes upon me now.

Heart Broken – (Check sadness and sorrow) Due to a lack of love. My heart is functioning at 100%. With each beat of my heart love radiates out and encompasses every area of my life.

Heart Problems – Due to tension filled life, and the inability to enjoy. Caught up in the world wind of production and the illusion of time and the game of life, trying to get ahead. Joy flows through me and this body and towards all those that love me and all those that I love.

Heartburn – (Check digestive enzymes, and check allergies) Due to fear, and the inability to digest life. Stockiness. Excessive acid. The process of life flows in, around and threw me now. It is safe to digest new ideas.

Hematochezia – see *Anus*

Hemorrhoids – Due to an inability to let go, and being burdened by the past. Inability to release that which serves us no longer. I release the past with love, there is more than enough time to accomplish what I need to in life.

Hepatitis A, B, C, E Other – (Check and clear liver weakness, viruses, allergies to blood, and self) Due to resentments and rage against the machine of life. My blood is 100% healthy and whole. All my organs, glands, and systems cooperate with each other. Going forward I am in harmony with life.

Hernia – Due to strains, pulling and overexertion. Organization coming undone. An inability to hold it all together. All my organs, glands and systems cooperate with one another. Synchronicity of life flows threw me now. Everything is as it should be.

Herpes Genitalia – (Check and clear viruses) Due to resentment and shame about one's self and sexuality. My sexuality is 100% normal and healthy. I have a high level of stamina. Weakness leaves my body as I read or hear this now. *Research high levels of vitamin c and L-lysine and vitamin Meyers IV's.*

Herpes Simplex – (Check and clear viruses) Due to stuffing of resentment and words, with an inability to speak up. Seething inside. Love and peace flow in, around and threw me. I speak only positive words. *Research high levels of vitamin c and L-lysine and vitamin Meyers IV's.*

Hips – Moving forward in life, seat of the soul. Ideal pacing of life, walk and gait. My gait and movement is perfectly structured for me in grace and ease. I move through life pain free.

Hip Problems – Due to fear of forward movement, fear of what will be found around the next corner of life. Feeling stagnant. My forward movement is ageless; grace and ease support this body.

Hirsutism – (Check hormones being out of balance and fish out) Due to an imbalance of the male and female energies. Playing the blame game, and an inability to accept nurturing. All my hormones are in balance. With grace and ease my body operates at peak efficiencies.

Hives – (Check liver and allergies, fish out the word hives) Due to a skin crawling, and irritation. An inability to process internally. I am at peace and I process internal and external pressure with grace and ease. Allergies are released from me as I read this now.

Hodgkin's Disease – (Check weakness of blood, fish out I have Hodgkin's) Due to feelings of being depleted and washed out. I have Hodgkin's (NO) I have learned all the lessons I needed to from it, having Hodgkin's still serves me (NO).

Holding Fluids – see *Fluid Retention, and Edema*. Due to a fear of loss and an inability to let go. Retaining water. Fish out fluid retention. Fish out inflammation. This body is in balance now. Fluids are processed with grace and ease. Stuck energy is released as I read this now.

Huntington's Disease – Due to an inability to change others, and or one's self. Feelings of being listless. The universe guides me, stabilizes me, and allows me to be at peace.

Hyperactivity – (Check and clear Shen disturbances, just these words) Due to racing thoughts and an inability to live moment by moment. My pressures have stabilized and feelings of self-worth return, and I am accounted for.

Hyperglycemia – (Check allergies to insulin and one's own blood sugar) Due to an inability to process the sweetness of life. Consistency rules the day, the ups and downs of life smooth out, here and now. I process sugars with grace and ease.

Hyperopia – see *Eye Disorders*. (Clear Eye Issues.)

Hypertension – (Check and clear for normalized blood pressure allow veins and arteries to function at 100% efficiency.) Due to an inability to go with the flow. My life is smooth, consistent and fun.

Hyperthyroidism – Due to feelings of being excluded. My thyroid functions at 100%, is healthy and whole, my temperature is regulated here and now.

Hyperventilation – (Check blood alkalosis) Due to an inability to trust the process and a lack of smooth. Lack of breath of life. It is safe and comfortable to breath in the breath of life with grace and ease.

Hypoglycemia – (Check blood sugar balance in body) Due to being overwhelmed. Inability to accept the sweetness of life. Life is joy filled. Smooth, and I am at peace.

Hypothyroidism – Due to having feelings of stifled, cold and stuck. Universal energies flow in, around and through me now. My body temperature is normalized.

Ileitis – see *Crohn's Disease*.

Impotence – (Check and normalize blood pressure and emotional weakness) Due to lack of strength, virility. Being weak. Inability to gather the strength of life and stand at attention. Inability to be strong like a bull. I am strong like a bull. I am potent. I am fertile and nourished. I am whole and driving forward as I read this now.

Incontinence – (Check bladder weakness and excessive amounts of bacteria. Fish out kidney weakness) Due to the inability to contain one's self and overflow of emotions. It is safe and comfortable for all my organs, glands and systems to work in harmony with one another.

Incurable – Due to hopelessness. Finality. Giving up on life. Lack of choice. It came out of the blue from the universe and can be returned as quickly as it came upon me. Miracles are a daily occurrence, and the universe guides my every move. Show me and tell me beyond all knowing that goodness can come from you.

Indigestion – (Check digestive enzymes) Due to the inability to listen to one's inner guidance. The assimilation process is positive and whole; everything comes together with goodness. *Research digestive enzymes and probiotics.*

Infection – (Check bacteria) Due to annoyance and being out of balance. It is safe and comfortable to be patient. This body has normalized all its processes and returns to homeostasis.

Inflammation – Due to irritated processes and thinking. Excessive pressure causing abnormal rising up. Damaged. I release all damages and pressures and I am healed and all is well as I read or hear this now.

Influenza – (Clear bacteria and viruses, fish out until no) Due to the need to withdraw from life, work and play. Stagnant. My body and temperature and processes have normalized as I read or hear this now.

Ingrown toenail/Podiatry/Foot Issues – (Check fungal infections) Due to being overly busy and ignoring self-care. It is safe and comfortable to take care of myself. I am now on equal footing, well-groomed and safe.

Injuries – (Check and clear inflammation) Due to being out of balance, mishaps and negative thinking. Balance comes upon me; my health is restored. I have licked the wounds of life and I am healed.

Insanity – (Check I am clear and running forward, change to yes) Due to separation from one's body, and reality. Inability to face childhood traumas. It is safe and comfortable for this body, mind and spirit to rejoin as one.

Insomnia – Due to overthinking, inability to feel safe and comfortable, worry and being unbalanced. I calm my mind and restful peace comes upon me. It is safe and comfortable to sleep. I am safe and all is well.

Intestinal Problems – (Check weakness of intestines and strengthen accordingly) Due to a lack of assimilation. I assimilate nourishment with grace and ease. All my internal organs are in harmony with one another as I read this now.

Itching – (Check and clear liver/skin) Due to being unsatisfied and uncomfortable in one's own skin. Apprehension. I know my place in the world. All my needs are met. I am safe now.

Itis – Due to inflammation of many different things, being out of balance and out of round. My world is not making sense. Normalizing relations with self and others, harmony comes upon us now.

Jaundice – (Check and clear liver, virus and bacteria) Due to being out of balance with one's own world. Backing up of waste. It is safe and comfortable to be in the flow of life and to have normalized temperature and blood flow as well as coloration.

Jaw Problems – Due to seething anger, resentment and seeking payback. It is safe and comfortable to relax and let go and let bygones be bygones. *Research cranial sacral chiropractic techniques.*

Joint Disorders – (Check water levels) Due to a lack of ease in movement and having a source of resistance and pain unknown. *Research MSM sulfate.*

Keratitis – see *Eye Disorders*. (Check and clear eye disorders, and eye strength) Due to an inability to see clearly or focus on what matters most. I now see my world through loving eyes, healthy and whole. My optical nerves and brain are in harmony with my eyes. *Research Lutein and Indium.*

Ketoacidosis – (Check and clear diabetes and kidney function. Check allergies to blood sugar and insulin and pancreatic weakness) Due to overwhelming sugar in the blood, and a burning of one's fat due to fear and the inability to process the sweetness of life. Fear of the future. It is safe and comfortable to have normal blood chemistries and all my body organs initiate process and complete with grace and ease.

Kidney Problems – (Check fear, and that kidneys functioning at 100%) Due to shame and fear overriding the body and causing restrictions. I release fear, judgement, shame and life's disappointments. In their place, I drop in joy and smooth. *Research kidney cleanses. Uva Ursi teas.*

Kidney Stones – (Check fear, anger, resentment) Due to formation of left over, unresolved disappointments and resentments. Fear accumulation. It is safe and comfortable to dissolve the past, be fully in the present and anticipate a bright future. *Research kidney cleanses.*

Knee Problems – (Check and strengthen tendons) Due to excessive pride and the inability to be flexible. Left knee can be moving forward in life problems. And Right knee can be feminine issues. Compassion rules the day. I feel supported and safe. I move and flex with the ebb and flow of life. *Research MSM and sulfur as well as glucosamine chondroitin. Test them for you.*

K (Potassium) Imbalances – (Check blood and water imbalances) Due to experiencing a life that is out of balance chemically, and blood that is out of balance. Arteries that feel restricted. Anger within the cells. My arteries and veins and blood flow with grace and ease. They are all in balance with one another. *Research supplements and hydration. Research IV Meyers Cocktails.*

Labor/Delivery – (Check and clear self, as well as baby, and treat them as an equal, separate person) It is safe and comfortable to conceive, carry and deliver this breath of life. I include my baby with each prayer as I breath, eat, and drink to positive I share this with my baby. *Research prenatal vitamins.*

Laryngitis – (Check for bacteria, virus, mold, fungus, mildew, yeast, candida, parasites or negative pathogens. Fish to No) Due to the inability to speak up, muted, and boiling anger. It is safe and comfortable to speak up. I am heard. My voice is strong. I am visible. *Research colors of mouth washes. Swish and gargle five times a day with the color that tests best for you. Can be red, green, yellow, blue, purple, or gold.*

Left Side of Body Issues – (Check feminine issues) Due to famine challenges or issues and conflict in your world how you see it. It is safe and comfortable to move forward in life. All my organs, glands, and systems operate in harmony with one another. People having left or right sided constant tendencies need physical touch, chiropractic, massage, acupuncture take your pick.

Left Sided Heart Failure – (Check inflammation and feminine issues, as well as lineage of female family members) Due to restrictive blood flow, hurts and slights haunting one's self and one's kindness. My heart pulls through, and beats with harmony. It processes the flow of life with grace and ease.

Leg Problems – (Check and clear circulation and low back issues) Due to a fear of moving forward and imbalance of emotions. Instability. My gate is strengthened, I feel supported, Life is steady.

Leprosy – Due to an inability to get or remain clean. Deep seated resentment and anger. I see and renew a life filled with love and hope. It is safe and comfortable to be included and experience my safe place in this world.

Leukemia – (Check and clear blood and joints and strength of bone marrow) Due to anger on the foundational, cellular level. Deep rejection of self. Harmony and balance flow in, around and through me. My blood, bones, joints and marrow are in symphony with one another as energy comes upon me now. *Research any tonics, vitamins, minerals, and herbs that boost the immune system.*

Leucorrhea – see *female problems.*

Liver Problems – (Check and clear anger and resentment and effects of eyes) Due to internal dialog that is filled with turmoil and regret. Anger at how one's life is going. I reach a balance in life and I have released anger, replacing it with joy, laughter and entertainment.

Lockjaw – (Check and clear inflammation, bones and joints) Due to deep seated tension, and a feeling of unresolved conflict. I release all past life influences, controlling the here and now. Tension flows out of my jaw, down threw my body leaving threw my feet into the ground as I hear or read this now.

Lump in Throat – (Check and clear bacteria) Due to stifling of one's emotions, and lose of voice. Inability to speak up. I am safe and I trust the process of life. It is safe and comfortable for me to speak up. Negative influences leave me now. *Research different mouthwash colors and use the one that tests best for you.*

Lung – (Check and clear inflammation and circulation, as well as virus and bacteria) Due to a deep-seated depression blocking the clear flow of oxygen into the body. A cloud overhead. I take in the fullness of life, breathing in clear energy, and breathing out negativity. All blocks are released from me now. *Research www.jimhumble.org and MMS2.*

Lupus – (Check and clear allergies to one's self, and clear your blood) Due to overwhelming self-sabotaging thoughts and ideas. Being allergic to one's self. It is safe and comfortable to be me. I can speak up for myself and I am worthy.

Lymph Problems – (Check and clear virus and bacteria) Due to the rain gutters of the house of my body being clogged. Clear this statement to no. My glands, organs and systems communicate and operate with peak corporation. Flowing with grace and ease, here and now. *Research lymph draining massage.*

Malaria – (Check and clear everything, malaria is the perfect storm of everything negative) Due to nature overcoming and consuming me. I am experiencing a return to homeostasis and balance of this body as all organs, glands and systems function as one. All foreign invaders have been driven out and released. *Research www.jimhumble.org and MMS1 and MMS2. Google Red Cross Study with Jim Humble.*

Mastitis – see *Breast Problems*. (Clear the word Mastitis.)

Mastoiditis – (Check and clear virus and bacteria, swelling, and inflammation) Due to an inability to understand because the volume of resistance and resentment is up to high. All my bones, joints, tendons, ligaments, and fascia corporate together in unison and work with each other. They are the ideal size and weight for this body. *Research MSM plus Sulfur.*

Measles/Mumps – (Check and clear all viruses) Due to weakened immunity to life and being overwhelmed by negative pathogens; a lack of life force. The life force within me is strengthened by the minute and releases all negativity holding me down. *Research www.jmhumble.org.*

Meningitis Bacterial or Viral – (Check and clear bacteria and virus, it can switch or be both, clear fever) Due to feelings of giving up. Being extremely overwhelmed by bacteria and virus. The feeling of being eaten alive. I recover and I am fully operational again. This body is in harmony and balance. All foreign invaders have been subdued. *Research www.jimhumble.org and MMS2.*

Menopause Problems – see *Female Problems.* (Check and clear change of life) Due to the feeling of having no self-worth, and an inability to give birth or contribute, Feelings of approaching the end of one's life. Clear this statement: As I go through the stages of life every day is filled with grace and ease, joy and laughter, regardless of this body's status. I am at peace with myself. I contribute.

Menstrual Problems – see *Female Problems.* Due to the rejection of one's famine attributes. Feelings of shame and being unclean. It is safe and comfortable to be a woman. All this body's processes are filled with grace and ease. I contribute. I am a goddess.

Metabolic Problems – (Check and clear metabolism) Due to an inability to process nutrition for fuel and sustenance all the way through the waste cycle. I intake nutrients and liquids and utilize them with grace and ease for optimal performance. *Research digestive enzymes and probiotics in-between lunch and dinner.*

Migraine Headaches – (Check dehydration, sensitivity to light, heat and cold. Clear this) Due to stressed tension and feelings of being overworked and unloved causing shut downs. I reenlist in life, with feelings of balance, grace and ease.

Miscarriage – (Check and clear female issues) Due to the fear of life and latent fear of adding on to the family. I feel divinely guided by spirit. Time heals all wounds. The process of life gives me hope for a new beginning.

Mononucleosis – (Check and clear bacteria and virus) Due to feeling unappreciated and let down by others. Feelings of being washed out and overcome. It is safe and comfortable to practice self -care. I am whole and all is well.

Motion Sickness – (Check and clear phobias) Due to feelings of being out of control and out of balance. I feel safe and at ease. Smooth and steady motion allows me to function; I return to the balance of nature.

Mouth Problems – (Check and clear bone, muscle, ligament, tendon, jaw, teeth, gums, roots, bacteria and virus) Due to inability to speak up and avoiding self-care. Harboring resentments. It is safe and comfortable for me to speak my peace, and to care for myself and others equally. I return to a full spectrum of health. *Research colors of mouthwashes and test which one works best for you.*

Multiple Sclerosis – (Check and clear and strengthen the myelin sheath of neurons and allergies to them and fascia of the body, bone, muscle, ligament, tendon, and joints) Due to this body feeling defeated by life. Hopelessness consumes me and I have given up on enjoyment of life. There is hope for me. I can recover, I can overcome. The health of this body can be restored. *Research high fat diets.*

Muscular Dystrophy – (Check and clear muscles) Due to feeling weak and washed out about this body and this life. Feelings of being unsupported. The breath of life inspires me and strengthens my every move. My muscles, bones, ligaments and fascia operate in symphony and harmony supporting one another. *Research high protein and high good fat diets.*

Myalgic Encephalomyelitis – see *Epstein-Barr virus. Research www.jimhumble.org and MMS2.*

Myocardial Infraction – see *Heart Attack.* (Fish out this word) Due to the heart stopping to work with the body. This heart rejoins this body in functioning. Perfect harmony and health surround me now.

Myopia – see *Eye Problems.* Due to an inability to trust the future and feeling unsafe in the now. Denying what is seen. I see with clear eyes. My eyes and optical nerves and brain function efficiently, healthy and whole.

Nails/Nail Biting – Due to nervousness, and fear of the past, present and future. Positive energy flows in around, and through me now. Stability and forward movement provide me with balance.

Narcolepsy – (Check and clear seizure disorders, and knowing the difference between being asleep and being awake) Due to checking out and fear of fully engaging in life. Unaware of knowing the difference of being awake and being asleep and what is appropriate. I know the difference between being asleep and awake and it is now safe and comfortable for me to be awake and conscious. I am fully engaged in life. *Research mineral deficiencies and high fat diets.*

Nausea – (Fish out the word, check and clear dehydration and motion sickness) Due to being out of balance and fearful experiences that cause weakness. I am in balance with life and all my processes of digestion are filled with grace and ease. My head, heart and stomach love one another. Apprehension leaves me now.

Nearsightedness – see *Eye Disorders and Myopia.* (Clear the word nearsightedness.)

Neck Problems – (Check and clear oxen yolk and financial struggles) Due to the inability to support the head and brain. Feelings of lack of family support. I feel supported, I am financially stable. I am moving through life with grace and ease.

Nephritis – (Check and clear kidney issues, and fear) Due to fear and resentment keeping me stuck and grounded. Circulation of life and fresh energy comes upon me and strengthens me now. I move forward with great strides of grace and ease. *Research www.jimhumble.org MMS2.*

Nervous System Disorders – (Check and clear nerve endings, stress, tension, anxiety and arteries) Due to overthinking and having too much electrical stimulation in the body. Feeling wired and out of sorts. Grace and ease flow in, around and through me now. Smoothness comes upon me now. I am at peace.

Neuralgia – (Clear and see Pain)

Neuropathy – Due to excessive communication, and being overly informed about the world. Living in fear. Overthinking. My world is a peaceful place. Smoothness comes upon me now. Life is a tai chi move.

Nodules – Due to inflated ego over career and status. A need to overly control. It is safe and comfortable to just let go and allow spirit and allow life. Things will turn out better than I had hoped if I can just let go of how I think it should be. I let go and I let God.

Nose Problems – (Check and clear allergies, bacteria, virus, mold, mildew, yeast, parasites, and negative pathogens) Due to an inability to breath freely in life. Inability to smell the goodness of life. I smell and breath clearly now. I smell and breath in the breath of life clearly now.

Numbness – (Check and clear blocks) Due to lack of circulation, an imbalance of temperature in life and blood flow. Every part of this body flows with grace and ease. Feeling is restored in all extremities.

Operation Problems (During) – (Check and clear the surgeon, team and operating room. Make sure all is running forward and clear) Due to lack of harmony, inability to be on track and go by the book, and inability to follow numbers, letters and processes in their succession. Everything flows with grace and ease; harmony is restored and I call upon the highest powers of the holy spirits and to guide the surgeons hand. Teams of love ones who have crossed over before me supervise this procedure.

Osteomyelitis – (Check and clear bones, bone marrow and inflammation) Due to an unstructured life that feels unsupported causing one to harbor frustrations, hurts, anger and resentment. My bones support me. They are strong, wholesome and well. Every aspect of this body is filled with grace and ease.

Osteoporosis – (Check and clear bones and the inability to retain calcium) Due to lack of structure and the inability to have an organized life. I have enough structure to create forward progress. My life is balanced between stiffness and apathy.

Ovaries – see *Female Problems/Disorders*.

Overweight – (Check and clear virus, bacteria, mold, mildew, yeast, fungus, parasites and negative pathogens) Due to stuffing, looking to armor the body for protection, out of fear.

It is safe and comfortable to be at my ideal weight for my height and body type. I know at some point I crossed that point. I have the reference point to get back to that weight as I hear and read this now. *Research digestive enzymes and probiotics.*

Paget's Disease – see *Breast Disorders*. Due to lack of care, and having a structure built on sand. Inability to create forward motion. My bones are safe, strong, forever renewing one another with grace and ease.

Pain – (Check and clear nerves and inflammation) Dee to imbalance of life and living, can be from shock, awe, or interface of normality. Could be a burn, cut, scrape, swelling, throbbing. This body is restored to health and wellbeing. It is safe and comfortable to be pain free. Pain does not have to be my new normal. I can be pain free.

Palsy Disorders – Due to being stuck in paralysis. A feeling of sinking in quicksand. Stuck and stymied. My life flows with grace and ease. This body is highly functioning and has a reference point to return to normality.

Pancreatitis – (Check and clear virus, bacteria, fever, blood and sugar) Due to angry and inflamed cells, swollen disorder and discomfort in life. All my organs glands and systems accept one another. They are within normal range and size.

Paralysis – (Check and clear chaos, drama, frozen in time) Due to being stuck, stymied, and shocked. It is safe and comfortable to move forward with grace and ease. Every aspect of life flows easily.

Parasites – (Check and clear parasitic infections, and those who are eating and using me up) Due to being overly used again and again. Feeling destroyed from the inside out. *Research www.jimhumble.org MMS2. Parasite cleanses. Hydro colon therapy.*

Parkinson's Disease – (Check and clear myelin sheath and allergies to proteins and one's self) Due to reflection upon one's life and feelings about lack of success. Strength and ease come upon me now. I feel supported, worthwhile, and my endurance increases with each passing hour.

Peptic Ulcer – (Check and clear bacteria, virus, and acid overflow) Due to excessive acid and the eating of one's self from the inside out. Normalcy comes upon me now. I am neither alkaline or acidic. I feel normal and I digest life with grace and ease. *Research BRAT-Bananas, wild or brown rice, applesauce, and toast. Bland diet and antibiotics if needed or colloidal silver or MMS2.*

Periodontitis – see *Gum and Mouth Disorders.*

Petit Mal Seizures – (Check and clear brain) Due to eruptions and sticking points that keep one stuck. Clear negative over-whelmed energies. This body runs and operates with grace and ease without any hiccups or disruptions. No more monkey wrenches thrown into the machine. Everything is smooth and well.

Pfeiffer's Disease – see *Mononucleosis.*

Phlebitis – (Check and clear vein weakness, blood, blood flow, and pressure) Due to being out of the flow of life, on the rocks, sitting on the sidelines. I am in the flow of life. All my veins, arteries and systems operate in unison.

Piles – see *hemorrhoids.*

Pimples – see *Acne.*

Pinkeye – (Check and clear bacterial infections) Due to the inability to see what life could offer. It is safe and comfortable to see with loving eyes. These eyes operate at 100% efficiency. My eyes, optic nerves and brain are in unison. *Research Similasan Eye Drops.*

Pituitary Gland Issues – (Check and clear, check organs glands and systems) Due to the closure of one's third eye Chakras are misaligned and out of focus. These organs, glands, and systems are in unison and harmony with one another.

Plantar Wart – (Check and clear fungus and bacteria) Due to an inability to move forward in life with grace and ease. My life has stubbed its toe on the rock of disappointment. The inability to feel planted on the earth. Alien feelings. I step forward in life, one foot in front of the other, pain free with grace and ease. *Research orthotics.*

Pneumonia – (Check and clear all garbage) Due to sorrow and sadness. Drowning in the negativity of life. I breath in the breath of life and I am restored. *Research www.jimhumble.org MMS1 or MMS2.*

Poison Ivy, Sumac, Oak, Nettle – (Check and clear allergies, bacteria and inflammation) Due to being lost in the forest. Unfamiliar surroundings. I resolve to quell and calm this inflammation and irritation with soothing grace and ease. *Research hydrocortisone creams and aloe. Use triple antibiotic ointment. There are a lot of things that can be found at the dollar store.*

Polio – (Check and clear family DNA, heredity, and past lives) Due to the inability to take life in stride and comfort. Having a body that is out of balance and off kilter, haphazard. My stride and walk is filled with grace and ease. Every part of this body operates in unison. I feel supported. Smooth. And I am moving forward in my life.

Postnasal Drip – (Check and clear sinus, nasal passages, bacteria and virus) Due to supressing childhood fears. I release and let go of all that serves me no longer. This body's temperature and moisture is with in balance. *Research Neti Pot, sauna therapy.*

Pre/Post Operational Problems – Due to hopelessness, fear, lack of trust in medicine and God. I enter in to this event with grace and ease knowing that this will improve my life. I will come out on the other side of this event better than ever.

> **Pre –** Align one's self, body, mind and spirit with everything working out fine. Check astrological times and moon phases. Avoid surgery during mercury retrograde.

> **Post –** It is safe and comfortable to recover and heal completely and fully. Check healing incision areas for drama, shock, and awe.

Pregnancy/Birth – (Check and clear conception, carrying to full term, create and give birth to a healthy baby) Due to fear of the unknown and that which I cannot see is inside me creating fear. I am a goddess, a nurturer and a giver of life. Spirit breaths in my direction and create all anew. *Research prenatal vitamins, juicing and eating clean.*

Premenstrual Syndrome – see *Female Problems.* (Check and clear allergies to blood and to gender) Due to confusion, fear of rejection. Inability to process life. It is safe and comfortable to be a woman and to be in the flow of life and to have body processes that are filled with grace and ease.

Prostate Problems – (Check and clear all negative pathogens) Due to a fear of aging, guilt feelings around masculinity, and an inability to be virile. All my organs, glands and systems are healthy at the ideal size and inflammation free. *Research pumpkin seeds and saw palmetto.*

Pruritus – see *Itching*. (Clear this word.)

Psoriasis – (Check and clear allergies to self, skin and liver) Due to an inability to accept responsibility. Skin is always due to liver. A clear, healthy liver equals clear healthy skin. My skin is healthy whole and held together in a smooth fashion. *Research hydro colon therapy.*

Psychiatric Illness – (Check and clear the name of the diagnosis, make sure clear is yes, running forward is yes) Due to being unclear, past emotional childhood traumas, past life chaos and drama, as well as family DNA, ancestral issues, and chemical dependencies. My body, mind and spirit are one. My brain is healthy and whole. I am free of all negative alien to me people, place and things. *Research supplements, GABA, Lithium Sulfate, St. John's Wart, 5HTP, Bacopa, Kava Kava, Menstat a brand of Himalayan Herbs product, passion flower and magnolia or relora bark. If you are taking any psychotropic prescriptions from a healthcare provider you will want to fish out; pull, delete and cancel any negative side effects caused by them. Test and clear. Any positive attributes for the prescription need to be strengthened..*

Pubic/Pelvic Bone Problem – (Check and clear blunt force trauma) Due to emotional, sexual, chaos and drama usually caused by accident or the attraction to trauma. The reproduction of life is safe and comfortable for me. I am safe, solid and strong.

Pyelonephritis – (Check and clear virus, bacteria, ureter/genital, bladder, kidneys and urea) Due to harboring of resentment and unclean, impure thoughts. Lack of self-care. I am clean, whole and safe. All my organs, glands and systems operate efficiently. *Research UVA URSI (bear berry).*

Quinsy Peri Tonsillar Abscess – see *Tonsillar Disorders.* (Check and clear bacteria, mold, mildew, yeast, candida, fungus, parasites and negative pathogens) Due to harboring resentments of anger, fear, and the inability to speak up (Stuffing). It is safe and comfortable to ask for my needs to be met and for me to have high levels of self-care. *Research and test for all colored mouth washes and which one will work best for you. Everyone seems to resonate with a different color.*

Rabies – (Clear this word) Due to anger, feelings of the need to be attacked or to attack. Extreme aggression. I release aggression, outrage and anger. Peace and calm come upon me now. *Research Zoonotic diseases. www.jimhumble.org MMS2.*

Rash – (Check and clear liver and skin and all negative pathogens) Due to delays and over reacting. My skin is 100% healthy, whole and free of negative pathogens. My skin is smooth and irritation free. *Research calamine, hydrocortisone cream, Epsom's salt lotions and aloe vera plants.*

Rectum – see *Anal Problems.*

Renal Problems – (Check and clear kidneys, virus, bacteria and all negative pathogens) Due to an innate fear of everything. All my organs, glands, and systems operate with grace and ease. I liver fearless and process fluids with ease. *Research MMS2, Cranberry, lemon in water and an alkaline diet, and kidney cleanses.*

Respiratory Problems – (Check and clear all negative pathogens, sinus/nasal/bronchial pathways and lungs) Due to feeling shut down, elephant on the chest, and the inability to breath in the goodness of life. I breath in the breath of life and it fills me with energy. I expand physically, mentally, and spiritually. The breath of life sustains me.

Rheumatism – (Check and clear joints and inflammation) Due to lacking in the department of love, stiffness in life I am flexible and I move with grace and ease free of frustration, stubbornness, and inflexibility. *Research cleanses and glucosamine chondroitin and MSM with sulfur and MMS2. (Test which will work best for you).*

Rheumatoid Arthritis – **(**Check and clear autoimmune diseases) Due to intentionally sabotaging and attacking one's self. Every aspect of my being is in harmony and every part of me functions at 100% and in harmony with every other part and all is well. *Research cleanses and glucosamine conjoining and MSM with sulfur and MMS2. (Test which will work best for you).*

Rickets – (Check and clear all negative pathogens, and vitamin c deficiency or the ability to absorb) Due to insecurities of the emotions and lack of loving kindness. My life is in balance. I love myself. Others love me. *Research Vitamin C therapy.*

Right Side of Body Weakness – (Check and clear the words, strengthen the same) Due to issues with the male figure and an inability to be grounded, and feeling as if one is an alien on earth. I feel grounded, secure and my masculine and feminine sides are in balance here and now. Harmony flows in around me now.

Right Sided Heart Failure – (Check and clear veins, arteries, blood and circulation and negative pathogens) Due to blockage and inflammation in love. The inability to love and be loved. This heart functions at 100% efficiency. Love flows in, though, and around my veins are arteries and body systems. My heart beats with love.

Ringworm – (Check and clear fungus and parasites) Due to a feeling of repeatedly running around in circles. Life runs smooth and forward, free of interruptions as I read or hear this now.

Root Canal – (Check and clear bacteria and all negative pathogens) Due to festering of resentment. Filled with fear. Feelings of listlessness and the inability to anchor ones' insecurities with love. A fresh new foundation is anchored within me, full of love, joy and ease. Restriction free.

Rounded Shoulders – (Check and clear DNA and family lineage and heritage of this issue. Check joints and tendons) Due to helplessly being stuck in a place of no return. Inability to carry the weight life. My body rises as well and structured, poised, and I carry myself with ease and joy. *Research chiropractic and cranial sacral therapy.*

Rubella – (Check and clear virus and bacteria) Due to an outbreak of emotional trauma and drama. The wish to die. It is safe and comfortable to thrive and be healthy. I am in the flow of life when healing frequencies comes through me now. *Research www.jimhumble.org MMS1 and MMS2.*

Sagging Lines – Due to a mind that is sagging and lagging. It is safe and comfortable to live a life in smooth. I absorb moisture with grace and ease. *Research Aloe Vera in the raw for a moisturizer. Bulletproof coffee.*

Scabies (Check and clear liver and skin and negative pathogens) Due to constant irritation from others. Making one's skin crawl. My skin is smooth as silk. My liver functions at 100% efficiency and all is well.

Sciatica – (Check and clear misalignments, pinched nerves) Due to self-sabotage and allowing back stabbing from others. Also, can be blunt trauma or impact. Good surrounds me. Safety is the word of the day. Everything this body uses is aligned and harmony as I read or hear this now. *Research chiropractic and cranial sacral therapies.*

Scleroderma – (Check and clear genetics, DNA and history of this disease. Check and clear sugars and parasites and yeast) Due to an inability to trust and allow time for self-care and preservation. Ignoring the obvious. The river of life flows with grace and ease. It is safe and comfortable to just be me. All aspects of this body are in harmony with each other and in the flow of life as spirit handles this in my favor. *Research high fat diets and www.jimhumble.org MMS2.*

Scoliosis – (Check and clear joints, family DNA, genetics and inheritance) Due to life sticking me. Painful life and immobility in life. This body is filled with grace and ease; freedom of movement rules the day. All parts of this body are fluid. *Research chiropractic and cranial sacral therapies.*

Scratches – (Clear accident prone and being hazardous) Due to feelings that life is irritating and a rip off. Every aspect of this life flows with grace and ease free of irritation.

Seasickness – see *Motion Sickness.* (Test and clear this word.)

Seizure Disorders – (Check and clear neuropathways and myelin sheaths, family DNA, and genetics) Due to wanting to flee from life. Braking the moments in time. It is safe and comfortable to be in this body. Everything is well, calm and grounded. Smooth flows threw me allowing moments to flow uninterrupted. *Research high good fat good lipid diets, CBD cannabis oil.*

Senility – (Check and clear DNA, family, genetics, of this life and others. Check negative pathogens) Due to feelings of confusion and an inability to cope with life, or to be fully present. It is safe and comfortable to be fully present, utterly aware, and engaged in life.

Sepsis – (Check and clear bacteria expelling negative pathogens into the veins) Due to feeling like crap and being undeserving. The blood of life flows threw me now, 199% healthy and whole, my veins and arteries work in unison. Homeostasis returns to me as I read or hear this now. *Research www.jimhumble.org MMS2.*

Shin Weakness/Pain – Due to ideas that have broken down and lack of self-worth. It is safe and comfortable to be me and have high self-worth. The energy of the universe supports me as I read or hear this now.

Shingles – (Check and clear virus, and the word shingles.) Due to feelings of being brought down by a foreign invader. An underlived liver, and resentments. The blood of life flows in, around and through me now. I am 100% healthy and all negative blocks in my path have been cleared. *Research MMS2. Liver cleanses.*

Shock – (Check and clear dehydration) Due to the inability to be safe in one's own body, checking out. Having disbelief. This body, mind, spirit and consciousness is fully awake, alive and vibrant. *Research electrolyte imbalances. Myer's Cocktail.*

Shoulder Problems – (Check and clear tendons and joint inflammation and all weakness) Front of shoulder is future, back of shoulder is past and top of shoulder is present. Due to resentment and carry the weight of the world. Financial setbacks of past, present or future. The spear of negativity that had stuck me is pulled out and removed. I am patched up and back in the game of life. Strength returns to me now.

Sickle Cell Anemia – (Check and clear blood, veins and arteries, DNA, history of family and all negative pathogens and the word) Due to a misshapen view of life. Blockage in the universal flow of life. The energy of life flows in, around and through me now. 100% health and wellbeing is mine.

Sinus Problems – (Check and clear sinus allergies and nasal pathways, clear all negative pathogens) Due to feelings of being shut down, the inability to breath in the breath of life. I breath in the breath of life with grace and ease. Unobstructed. *Research MMS2.*

Skeletal Problems – (Check and clear bones, bone marrow, and structure) Due to a lack in structure, and feelings of weakness and unsettledness. Structure and organization returns to me now. Every aspect of this body operates in unison. *Research allergies to calcium and vitamin D Blood Iron Ferritin levels.*

Skin Problems – (Check and clear allergies to one's self and liver) Due to feelings of upsets that are internalized and rise to the surface irritating the skin. My skin is smooth as silk, feeling protected and whole. *Research bulletproof coffee. Coconut oil.*

Slipped Disc – (Check and clear inflammation, joints, and nervous system) Due to lack of structure often caused by negative impact or shock. I am realigned, reinvigorated, structurally sound and all is well. *Research chiropractic and cranial sacral and healing mats of jade or amethyst therapies. Test what is best for you.*

Snoring – (Check and clear nasal, sinus, bronchial and lungs) Due to the inability to breath in the breath of life with grace and ease. The rhythm of life flows in and through me now. It is safe and comfortable to sleep peacefully now. When I am awake, I am awake, when I am asleep I am asleep. Everything is well. *Research black seed.*

Solar Plexus – Due to a blockage between you and that intuitive gut feeling. Stockiness. I am open and receptive to receive messages from spirit. I remain steadfast and mighty. *Research cranial sacral and chiropractic therapies.*

Sore Throat – (Check and clear all junk and negative pathogens) Due to stuffing and the inability to speak up. Suppressing what I would like to say out of fear. It is safe and comfortable for me to be myself, and find my voice, and speak my peace without fear of repercussions. *Research every color of mouthwash and test which is best for you. Gargle with it 5 times a day.*

Sores – (Check and clear all negative pathogens) Due to an outside negative source coming down upon me. I breath in the well spring of life. This body functions at 100% health and wellbeing. Any negative issue is dispelled. *Research and test different ointments.*

Spasms – (Check and clear muscles, and electrolyte imbalances) Due to sporadic issues and being out of rhythm with life. It is safe and comfortable to release and relax. My life is balanced now. *Research magnesium and hydration.*

Spastic Colitis – see *Colon.*

Spinal Curvature – (Check and clear DNA, bones, muscles, ligaments, tendons, joints and family history) Due to inability to have a structured life, inability to be supported by life and feeling abandoned by spirit. I stand erect and tall. I am aligning with life and living with purpose. *Research chiropractic and cranial sacral therapies.*

Spinal Meningitis – see *Bacterial and Viral Meningitis.*

Spleen Problems – (Check and clear blood, dampness, all negative pathogens) Due to irrational obsessions and over-thinking. Self-sabotage and the inability to let go. I trust all my organs, glands and systems to cooperate with each other in the process of living and life. *Research acupuncture.*

Sprains – (Check and clear inflammation) Due to resistance to change. Directional mishaps and stockiness. My life is on track and moving forward with grace and ease.

Sterility – (Check and clear the inability to reproduce and clear the body being at war with itself. Clear arguments between romantic partners) Barren. Due to a disinterest in creating a new life. It is safe and comfortable for me to move forward in life contributing to all others and finding solace in tis.

Stiff Neck – (Check and clear being unsupported) Due to wearing the oxen yolk. Financial stresses. My financial stress is released and I feel supported in my spiritual life. Stress and tension leave me now. *Research chiropractic and cranial sacral therapies as well as acupuncture.*

Stiffness – Due to rigidity and the inability to change one's mind. Stuck thinking. I flow with grace and ease and I am open to alternative ideas and suggestions free of judgement. *Research DMSO and sulfur creams. Use icy hot and Epsom's salt baths. Magnesium.*

Stomach Problems – (Check and clear digestive enzymes, parasites, H-pylori and negative pathogens) Due to fear of the future and the inability to assimilate nutrients and the goodness of life. It is safe and comfortable to assimilate nutrients and to be in the pulse of life. *Research probiotics in-between lunch and dinner.*

Stroke/CVA – (Check and clear brain, blood, heart and lungs) – Due to a sudden stockiness and refusal to change. A stop in the flow of life. It is safe and comfortable to acknowledge change, to access change, and to be a part of change without it harming me. *Research cranial sacral therapies, chamomile tea, 5HTP, L-theanine.*

Stuttering – (Check and clear brain and speech imbalance and lack of cadence) Due to an inability to cry or speak up for one's self. Brain is out of sync with speech. Communications come to me easily and effortlessly and all is well here and now. *Research GABA and high good lipid diet.*

Sty – (Check and clear all negative pathogens and allergies) Due to an anger towards someone that is clouding one's vision of a beautiful life. It is safe and comfortable to view everything with love and joy. *Research Similasan eye drops and Similasan eye allergy relief.*

Suicidal Intentions – (Check and clear negative entities and influences. Make sure the person is clear, and running forward because these will be out of whack) Due to refusal to see life in ways of beauty and splendor. A black cloud hanging over one's happiness. Feelings of impending doom and deep hurts and pains. There is always hope. I find something or someone to live for and to look forward to as I read or hear this now. *Research hormonal imbalances, test St. John's Wart. Kava Kava, L-theanine, 5HTP, GABA and lithium orotate. One of these or in combination can be a solution.*

Swelling – (Check and clear inflammation) Due to clogged beliefs and painful thoughts. It is safe and comfortable to return all functions to normal dimensions and sizes. All actions and interactions are in unison with one another. *Research magnesium and Epsom salt baths.*

Syphilis – (Check and clear virus and bacteria and all negative pathogens) Due to the need of personal protection. Self-sabotaging behavior. Clear shame. It is safe and comfortable to protect myself and to use caution in all my dealings. *Research penicillin treatment.*

Tapeworm – (Check and clear parasites) Due to people, places and things taking advantage of me and eating me from the inside out. This body is filled with grace and ease and operates at peak efficiencies without foreign or alien interferences. *Research www.jimhumble.org MMS2, wormwood black walnut hulls and cloves in combination. Avoid sushi and unclean salads, especially scallions.*

Teeth Problems – (Check and clear bacteria, bone weakness, and calcium deficiencies) Due to the inability to smile about life and to process foods and nutrients with grace and ease. A lack of structure in ones' life. This body is aligned, structurally sound, and processes all positive nutrients and fluids with ease. *Research different color mouth washes and test which will work best for you. Brush and floss regularly and after every meal!*

Temporomandibular Joint (TMJ) – (Check and clear negative weaknesses in joints, tendons, muscle and bone) Due to stress, over-thinking, and grinding one's teeth at life. I clear my DNA, my history, my family inheritance of all tension and stress. I chew pain free. *Research chiropractic, cranial sacral, and acupuncture therapies.*

Testicle Problems – (Check and clear all negative pathogens) Due to lack of virility and lack of reproduction. Lack of fertility.

Every day in every way I become stronger and my potency increases as I read or hear this now. *Research Tibulus.*

Tetanus (Lockjaw) – (Check and clear bacteria, virus and negative pathogens) Due to carelessness, and being off balance, off kilter and susceptible to foreign alien invaders. Fish this out to No. I am restored to a high level of health and well-being. This body is healthy and whole. *Research www.jimhumble.org MMS2.*

Throat Problems – (Check and clear all negative pathogens) Due to the inability to speak up for one's self. Stuffing the truth and fear of reprisal. It is safe and comfortable to have my voice of reason restored. I speak up for myself without fear of criticism. *Research different colored mouth washes and test which works best for you.*

Thrush – (Check and clear all negative pathogens) Due to an overindulgence of the sweetness of life. It is safe and comfortable to have boundaries and balance in all that I say and do, and in all that I consume. *Research different colored mouth washes and test which works best for you. And clear and refrain from excessive sugar.*

Thymus – (Check and clear propensities towards tumor. Clear all negative pathogens) Due to everything and everyone seeming to be after me. Safety and calm flow in, around, and through this body. *Research Sea Kelp.*

Thyroid (Hyper and Hypo) – (Check and clear all negative pathogens) Due to the inability to see the good and feeling as if I am sitting on the sidelines of life. The temperature is in balance, all organs, glands, and systems are in harmony, here and now. *Research Indium and Sea Kelp.*

Tic, Twitches, Tremors – (Check and clear electrical imbalances and negative synapse firings and mishaps.) Due to uncontrollable to reset and start over with this body's functions and purposes. It is safe and comfortable to be on track fully functioning, here and now. *Research magnesium, GABA, and Tai Chi, Chi Gong and Yoga.*

Tinnitus – (Check and clear the kidneys, and being off balance and every component of the ear, make them in harmony with the brain) Due to blocking out that which I do not want to hear and words I feel would harm me. I hear with grace and ease, clearly and effectively.

Toe Problems – (Check and clear bone, muscle, tendon and joints as it is usually a joint issue) Due to lack of balance, inability to feel rounded and the inability to move forward in life. Stagnation and stockiness. I move forward with grace and ease. In balance. In harmony. It is safe just to be me. *Research glucosamine chondroitin and orthotics.*

Tongue Problems – (Check and clear muscles) Due to the twisting of words, an inability to speak up, or saying too much. It is safe and comfortable to speak up for myself without fear of repercussions. *Research mouthwash colors and test which works best for you. Look up allergies.*

Tonsillitis – (Check and clear bacteria and virus and all negative pathogens) Due to the inability to speak up and feelings of being put down. Creatively challenged. It is safe and comfortable for me to be clear, and speak up and to have a body that is 100% healthy and whole. *Research mouthwash colors and test which works best for you. Explore gargling with warm Sea Salt.*

Tuberculosis – (Check and clear bacteria and the lungs and bronchial pathways and breathing as well as sinus and nasal passages) Due to drifting, purposelessness, and feeling put upon by life. Wanting revenge. It is safe and comfortable to live in peace and to give and receive love. I experience a purpose filled life as I read or hear this now. *Research www.jimhumble.org MMS2. Research blackseed and test how many you should take a day.*

Tumors – (Check and clear and clear past life disturbances and all negative pathogens as it is some odd mixture of them) Due to excessive anger or resentment and fear that has stopped me in my tracks just at the sound of the word. Deep fears around future life and living. I move forward through life healthy and whole. It is safe and comfortable for me to thrive in this lifetime and contribute to others. *Research MMS2 www.jimhumble.org.*

u

Ulcers – (Check and clear all negative pathogens) Due to feelings of being eating up by time, anger, resentment, fear, guilt and shame that has been turned inward. Cleanliness washes over me and restores this body to optimum health and all is restored. *Research MMS2 www.jimhumble.org and coconut oil and high good lipid diets.*

Urethritis – (Check and clear negative pathogens) Due to being and feeling pissed off and inflamed and irritated with life. The rivers of life and this body flow with grace and ease as I hear or read this now. *Research Uva Ursi (Bear Berry) and cranberry juice and MMS2.*

Urinary Bladder Infections – (Check and clear negative pathogens.) Due to anger towards ones' romantic partner. This body flows with grace and ease, all functions flow in harmony as I hear or read this now. *Research Uva Ursi (Bear Berry) and cranberry juice and MMS2.*

Urticaria – see *Hives and Allergies.* (Check and clear this word.)

Uterine Disorders – see *Female Problems.* (Check and clear all negative pathogens) Due to the inability to enjoy life and reproduce life. A disconnected universe. The universe and the goddess of life come together as one and create the way for spiritual miracles. *Research Black Cohosh, Loalsan Douche, Maca root, red raspberry leaf tea, and horny goat weed.*

Vaginitis – see *Female Problems*. (Check and clear all negative pathogens.) Due to punishment, resentment, self-loathing and seething anger at a romantic partner. Out of the flow of life. This body is in the flow of life. Every aspect of this body functions at 100% efficiency and is strong. *Research Loalsan Douche.*

Varicella (Chicken Pox) – (Check and clear these words, virus, bacteria and all negative pathogens) Due to the feeling and need to check out from life for a while and to be too sick to work or play. I see myself as healthy, whole and clear skinned. *Research aloe vera and baking soda for application. Liver cleanses (Skin can relate to liver).*

Varicose Veins – (Check and clear veins and the word) Due to excessive burdens and long standing hurts maintaining the same positions for long periods of time. My veins, arteries and blood all cooperate and are in harmony with one another and at the right pressure and flow for this body. *Research surgery if critical. Compression stockings, and vein eraser creams. Vitamin K and horse chestnut cream.*

Vasovagal Attack – (Check and clear the words, and all negative pathogens) Due to an imbalance in the pressures of life. This heart, blood pressure, veins and arteries all function together and are in balance and in harmony with one another. *Research Ayurveda heart medicines.*

Venereal Disease – (Check and clear all negative pathogens) Due to self-punishment and feelings of guilt and shame. Self-sabotage. It is safe and comfortable to love myself, to love others, and to allow others to love me. I am 100% healthy and disease free. *Research MMS2. www.jimhumble.org.*

Vertigo – (Check and clear the word, and inner ear and all negative pathogens) Due to a lack of balance and the world spins without me. It is safe and comfortable to have balance and a clear vision. Motion sickness also leaves me as I read or hear this now. *Research coconut oil and olive oil for the ears. Similasan ear drops.*

Viral Infections – (Check and clear virus and all negative pathogens) Due to feeling bitter and needing a break from the momentum of life. Feeling shut down. I am in the flow of life. It is safe and comfortable for me to make forward progress daily. I am healthy and whole and 100% online.

Vitiligo – (Check and clear skin, liver, family history and all negative genetic pathogens as well as autoimmune diseases.) Due to the inability to feel inclusive and longing to be a part of my people. A cast out and a cast away. This skin is smooth and all its pigment is in harmony. This body's liver functions at 100% efficiency. It is safe and comfortable to feel included with my tribe. *Research and clear myelin sheaths, cell DNA and high good lipid fat diets.*

Vomiting – (Check and clear all negative pathogens.) Due to being sick to my stomach over people, places, things, and situations. Calm comes upon me now. It is safe and comfortable to digest life. *Research BRAT diet (Bananas, wild rice, applesauce, rye toast), Ginger, and generic orange peanut butter crackers with a coca cola.*

Vulva – see *Female Problems.* (Check and clear this word and problem.)

W

Warts – (Check and clear liver, skin, fungus, mold and all negative pathogens.) Due to excessive dampness and mildew buildup in this body. This body operates with grace and ease and is free and clear of excessive dampness. My skin is smooth as silk. *Research compound-w. Bulletproof coffee. Liver cleanse.*

Weakness – (Check and clear frailty and all negative pathogens.) Due to a lack of energy and an inability to cope with life and checking out and sitting on the sidelines to avoid playing in the game of life. I feel invigorated. I thrive. I am back playing in the fun game of life. I am fully engaged in life. *Research B vitamins and a high good fat lipid diet.*

Whiteheads – see *Acne*. (Check and clear this word.)

Wisdom Teeth Pain – (Check and clear pain and negative pathogens.) Due to feelings of confinement. There is enough space for every aspect of me now. I am healthy and whole. All aspects of my life are welcome and useful here. *Research cloves, and used tea bags to relieve pain. Anbesol for temporary relief.*

Wounds – (Check and clear all negative pathogens.) Due to nursing deep hurts and an imbalance with life. Off Kilter and clumsy. I am restored to health and balanced and to a feeling of well-being. I am safe and grounded while still moving forward with grace and ease. I am restored.

Wrist Problems (Carpel Tunnels) – (Check and clear joint pain and gallbladder.) Due to negative energy stifling my grip to reach positive outcomes. A feeling of being cut off and a lack of flow in life. The flow of life easily moves in, around and through me now, nourishing my reach and my grasp and the extension of life itself. *Research gallbladder cleanses.*

X/Y/Z

X-Chromosomal Disorders – (Check and clear DNA, RNA and genetics as well as family, ancestral inheritance) Due to an incarnation that is less than complete, lacking the essentials of life and an inability to fully cope and function. Every aspect of my being comes together with grace and ease. I am complete, whole and well. I am highly functional and satisfied.

Y-Chromosomal Disorders – (Check and clear x-chromosomal, female DNA, RNA and genetics as well as family, ancestral inheritance) Due to issues with suffering, and being less than complete. Wanting to be left alone. Needing to be solitary for life. These sound harsh, but are from spirit and what needs to be cleared. It is safe and comfortable to be highly functional, and to allow the very essence of my being to be complete, whole, and sufficient in all areas of life. It is safe and comfortable to give and receive love as I read or hear this now.

Yeast Infections – see *Candida/Yeast*. (Check and clear this word.)

Zoonotic Diseases – (Check and clear parasites, viruses, bacteria off your pets.) Due to anger and frustrations between your animal human relationships. Miscommunications and misunderstandings. I feel the energy of love and communication between my human animal relationships. It is safe and comfortable to be in harmony between the animal kingdom and this human world without spreading disease, illness or disorder. We safely live together.

Questions?

I encourage you to have at least ONE session in person, or by phone or Skype. It could save you a lot of time and frustration which also equates to saving you money!

Jimmy Mack
Voice: 727.678.0557
Email: info@jimmymackhealing.com
http://www.jimmymackhealing.com/myliquidfish
www.twitter.com/myliquidfish
www.facebook.com/myliquidfish

My You Tube Channel:
https://www.youtube.com/channel/UC6dY61gWJhNOF_wwUnjC0iw

He sent his word, and healed them.   —*Psalms 107:20*

Free One Hour Live Video Healing Sessions with me.
Super Powers Video show interview:
http://goo.gl/EL7yIF

The Law of Attraction Radio Show Video interview:
http://goo.gl/6dra8i

In person, phone, and Skype Appointments worldwide
Skype: Jimmy.Mack55 Clearwater Florida USA

Jimmy Mack

Transformational Healing of Body, Mind and Spirit,
People, Places, Pets and Situations!

MyLiquidFish®   Change Made Simple®

About the Author

Jimmy Mack is a medical intuitive and spiritual life coach.

He works/plays with clients worldwide by way of in-person appointments, phone, and Skype. Jimmy Mack is an ordained minister, has degrees in American Studies, Theology, and he has a Doctorate in Divinity as well as a PhD in Metaphysics. He learned about Reiki and became a Mayan Usui Reiki Master. He has studied psychometry, and psychic development. He has gone on shamanic journeys; he has taken remote viewing classes and studied Ascension with the monks. Later, he explored and completed levels of Access Consciousness™, ThetaHealing™ as developed by Vianna Stibal, as well as levels one, two, and three of Reconnective Healing™ made popular by Eric Pearl DC. He became a certified practitioner in Matrix Energetics™ with Richard Bartlett DC, NP, as well as taking numerous courses of the Yuen Method™ made popular by Dr. Kam Yuen.

He has completed a variety of healing modalities but after a near death experience (NDE) he noticed that his ability to help and contribute to others had greatly increased.

Jimmy Mack has been given by spirit his own method of creating change now known as My Liquid Fish®.

Made in the USA
Lexington, KY
13 October 2017